mondofragil

MODER O JAPAN

mondofragile
modern fashion illustrators from japan
selected by Delicatessen

Happy Books, Italy

ISBN 88-86416-42-3

mondofragile © 2002 First published in Italy by Happy Books srl
Printed and bound in Italy by Grafiche Jolly - Modena
font: Chalet Comprimé by House Industries
english translation: Letizia Rustichelli, Maurizio Maestri
japanese translation: Manuel Majoli, Sai Tamiya

Concept:
cristiana valentini & gabriele fantuzzi
www.delicatessen.it

Art direction:
gabriele fantuzzi , delicatessen
gabriele@delica.it

Distribution:
www.happybookstore.com
happy@happybooks.it

Website:
www.mondofragile.com

Contact:
info@delica.it

page 1 and this page
tadahiro uesugi
illustration for japanese magazine
Photoshop

opposite
hitomi nagao
new year
artist's collection
ink, pen, Photoshop

contents

tada o[re]ba oru tote yuki no furi ni keri

c'ero soltanto.
c'ero...
intorno cadeva la neve.

Kobayashi Issa (1763-1828)

"Il colore giapponese, oltre che essere elegante e dolce, ha un'altra faccia abbastanza evidente. Innanzitutto i giapponesi hanno una percezione cromatica piatta, intuitiva, e apparentemente non vedono il colore con la luce come gli occidentali. Anche i toni forti, o quelli morbidi, più che i riflessi della luce e le ombre, si decidono in base al senso del colore che quell'oggetto possiede e in base alla percezione del colore. I principi estetici come iki, fascino sensuale, shibui, povertà discreta, hannari, brillantezza pacata, più che identificare una tonalità cromatica, raccontano spesso le emozioni dell'animo".

TANAKA IKKO

MONDOFRAGILE è un sogno diventato realtà. Questo libro ne è la sua forma compiuta, insieme alla mostra itinerante e al sito internet (www.mondofragile.com).
Il progetto prende vita dal desiderio, divenuto quasi una necessità, di rendere visibile l'immensa forza seduttiva di illustratori che vivono e lavorano in Giappone. Nell'occidente europeo molto sappiamo delle produzioni di Manga e Anime; poco o nulla invece conosciamo dell'illustrazione moderna realizzata nel paese del Sol Levante. E dire che spesso ci troviamo di fronte a lavori di qualità molto superiore ai nostri standard, ma forse la distanza e le difficoltà linguistiche sono da ostacolo ad una maggiore visibilità al di fuori dell'Estremo Oriente.

MONDOFRAGILE è soprattutto un omaggio alla cultura visiva del Giappone.
E' una dichiarazione d'amore incondizionato verso questa tradizione millenaria e la sua continua capacità di rinnovarsi ed ampliare i confini dei mondi visivi.
Il criterio di selezione degli illustratori presenti in questo libro è strettamente emotivo; abbiamo scelto immagini e figure che colpissero i nostri sensi, quelle dove l'effetto visivo, la percezione delle forme, la scelta cromatica, coinvolgesse la sfera emozionale piuttosto che quella logica. Al di là delle tecniche o dell'esperienza dei singoli abbiamo privilegiato una ricchezza espressiva e una personalità creativa ben definite per ogni artista; la stessa suddivisione in categorie è ampiamente soggettiva

Molto più di una massiccia compilation d'immagini, MONDOFRAGILE rappresenta un formidabile affresco sull'illustrazione contemporanea orientata alla moda.
I 24 artisti presentati sono in costante equilibrio tra forme-immagini giapponesi e fascinazione estetica euro-occidentale. I lavori scelti raccontano delle diverse forme di quotidianità, di spazi intimi e gesti ispirati; sono immagini che comunicano spesso una nostalgia di qualcosa di semplice. Questa "semplicità dell'intuizione" tipica della cultura giapponese diventa fonte d'ispirazione per chiunque si occupi di comunicazione, design o subisca il fascino delle arti figurative. Anche solo il piacere di guardare le oltre 400 illustrazioni di questo libro e di soffermarsi sulle più evocative può essere un'esperienza appagante verso la percezione di un mondo (fragile) condiviso.

DELICATESSEN

YUKA MAEDA
this page
totenkou
artist's collection
adobe illustrator

opposite
peony my love
artist's collection
adobe illustrator

tada o[re]ba oru tote yuki no furi ni keri

just existing
I exist...
snow flitting down.

Kobayashi Issa (1763-1828)

The Japanese colour is not only elegant, smart and delicate, it also shows another quite clear aspect. First of all Japanese people have an intuitive and flat chromatic perception and apparently they don't see the colour in the daylight as Westerners do. Even the deep and bright colours or the delicate and light ones - more then the glares of the lights and the shadows - are decided on the basis of the meaning of the colour that a particular object has or on the perception of it. The aesthetic principles like iki, sensual charm, shibui, discreet poverty, hannari delicate lightness do not identify a specific chromatic tone, but they often testify the emotions of the soul.

TANAKA IKKO

MONDOFRAGILE (FRAGILEWORLD) is a dream which has become true. This book together with the itinerary exhibition and the web site shows it in a complete form. The project moves its first steps from the desire and the need to show the immense seductive power of the illustrators living and working in Japan. In the European West a lot is known of Manga and Anime, but very little - if nothing – of the contemporary modern illustration of the Levant, although very often these works are of a very high quality, even superior to our usual standards.
Maybe the distance and the linguistic difficulty are an obstacle for a bigger visibility outside the Far East.

MONDOFRAGILE is above all a homage to the visual Japanese culture. It is an unconditional love declaration to that millenary tradition and to its continuous ability to renew and widen the borders of the visual world. The selection criterion of the artists represented in the book is strictly emotive; we have chosen images and pictures able to struck our senses, those where the visual effect, the perception of the forms and the chromatic choice involve more the emotional sphere then the logic one. Beyond the technical ability or the experience of each of the artists, we have favoured the expressive richness and the creative personality for each of them; the classification in the book is also amply subjective.

More then a massive compilation of images MONDOFRAGILE represents an incredible fresco on the contemporary illustration turned on fashion. The 24 artists involved in the book are in constant balance between Japanese forms/images and aesthetic Euro-Western fascination. The chosen works witness the different forms of daily life, of intimate space and inspired gesture; they are images often recollecting a nostalgia of something simple. This "Simplicity of Intuition" typical of the Japanese culture, becomes an inspiration source for all those involved in the communication field, design or for those simply attracted by the figurative art.
Having a look to the - more then 400 - images of this book and dwelling upon the most evocative ones can be a satisfying experience towards the perception of a shared (fragile) world.

DELICATESSEN

YUKA MAEDA ILLUSTRATION
FLAVOR GIRLS

Fonti, progetti, figure

di Carlo Branzaglia

chinatru souzen
kimono
artist's collection
Illustrator

Il ruolo delle fonti

Un libro come questo forse non ha bisogno di un contributo critico che ne rilegga il contenuto: una navigazione affascinata e affascinante fra un repertorio di immagini ben individuato. Ci permette però di fare innanzitutto qualche considerazione sul valore stesso che questi *source books* ricoprono nella costruzione di una cultura visiva, pragmaticamente (ma non solo) intesa. Certo il termine *source book* suona generico, in quanto può essere usato per definire una grande serie di proposte editoriali ormai configuratesi in un segmento di mercato proprio, con tipologie differenti che seguono finalità differenti, che vanno dall'aggiornamento all'ispirazione, finanche al brutale riuso. In questo senso, volumi di fonti (di immagini) accomunano tipologie diverse che vanno, solo per esemplificare, dagli annual (a scopo di aggiornamento); ai titoli che raccolgono immagini a tema (che siano cartoline o espositori punto vendita, a fine di ispirazione), ai cataloghi di decori o peggio alla clip art, oggi confinata nelle memorie del computer (che mirano a un riciclaggio con o senza manipolazioni dell'immagine di partenza). Questi prodotti editoriali, nelle differenti finalità, partono comunque dall'idea che l'immagine possa anche essere considerata un semilavorato da trattare, sia per interpretare i trend circostanti, sia per carpire elementi formali di base, sia per rimaneggiare invece patrimoni iconografici già configurati. Attività tutte in qualche modo necessarie a chi produce immagini. Questa visione sincronica si adatta a una situazione, sicuramente resa qui in maniera sintetica, dello stesso mercato, un mercato parallelo che ha fra i suoi utenti una comunità internazionale fatta di progettisti grafici, illustratori, pubblicitari, ma anche stilisti e designer di prodotto, perché no.

Se vogliamo divertirci a fare una lettura diacronica, invece, dovremmo forse considerare che i primi esempi di questa particolare proposta editoriale risalgono al celeberrimo The Grammar of Ornament, di OWEN JONES, pubblicato a Londra nel 1856. Il che peraltro ci obbliga a ricordare che il problema delle fonti è insito nella cultura del progetto: lo stesso libro di Jones rientra a pieno titolo (le date parlano da sole) in quel dibattito che portò allo sviluppo (in Gran Bretagna, in primis) della stessa cultura del design, nell'humus derivato dalle neonate esposizioni universali, nelle quali i prodotti fanno mostra di sé (e Jones stesso fu sovrintendente ai lavori della prima, a Londra nel 1851); dalla nascita dei musei di arti decorative (il Victoria and Albert fu fondato nel 1852), dallo stesso dibattito (parlamentare) sull'educazione al progetto. In attesa di una sintesi formale dalle Arts and Crafts.

Il testo visuale

Attenzione quindi a trattare con sufficienza questo settore: nella sua utilità pragmatica esso nasconde evidentemente una lettura che non si piega alla sola esigenza del sapere, ma anche a quella del saper fare. Forse Owen Jones questo problema l'aveva compreso: aveva compreso cioè la necessità di fornire semilavorati ai creatori di immagini "applicate" di allora, una categoria di professionisti in piena via di sviluppo. L'eco di questa comprensione del problema, in un contesto ovviamente molto mutato e dominato anche dalla necessità dell'offerta just in time (si vedano le quantità di volumi immediatamente dedicate al web design) la si ritrova nell'autorità di proposte come questa che andiamo introducendo. Senza paura di paragoni artificiosi, dobbiamo ricordare che l'ipotesi di una curatela prevede una interpretazione, una ottica, una lente attraverso la quale il materiale che si raccoglie viene organizzato. Attenzione, non è una novità assoluta, il fatto che volumi di immagini palesino un curatore che ne organizza i contenuti. Ma non ci siamo ancora seriamente soffermati a pensare a due elementi. Il primo riguarda la particolarità di organizzazione di un libro fatto con immagini, la sua capacità di trasferire informazioni, differente senz'altro dall'impianto strutturale di un volume concepito per la scrittura. Il secondo, la peculiarità culturale di un testo generato da un progettista (come sono CRISTIANA VALENTINI e GABRIELE FANTUZZI, nascosti dalla sigla del loro studio DELICATESSEN anche nella gestazione di questo volume); e usiamo vezzosamente la parola testo, tanto amata dalla semiotica, per ricordare che comunque qualunque forma di messaggio (anche quello visuale) rappresenta un testo da interpretare.

Certo i due aspetti sono collegati. Anzi, ad essere sinceri, la soluzione del problema l'aveva già data ALBERT STEINER nei suoi scritti (e siamo nel secondo dopoguerra) quando parlava della figura del "redattore grafico" segnalando (ante litteram) il ruolo di gestione dell'informazione da parte di chi si occupa della sua messa in pagina (della sua messa in scena). Frutto, ed esempio, di tale ipotesi è evidentemente Il Politecnico, la rivista diretta da ELIO VITTORINI, dove è smaccata l'importanza culturale (e politica) del progetto grafico. Nella qualità di un progetto grafico, noi stessi in realtà riconosciamo la sua capacità di trasferire informazioni nel rapporto fra testo ed immagine; e quando l'apparato iconografico si fa consistente (nelle riviste, nei libri, nei siti web) la sua cernita e la sua organizzazione spazio temporale sono fonti di trasmissione di significati. E delle migliori riviste di immagini, si è sempre detto che gli apparati iconografici erano in grado di esprimersi da soli, con il testo nel semplice ruolo di supporto, anche se utile.

Sapere e fare

La nota caratteristica di questo volume è che, progettato da progettisti per altri progettisti, esso usa armi comuni alla comunità dei designer. Armi tecniche (i formati, le didascalie, la qualità delle riproduzioni) e progettuali (la gabbia, l'impaginazione, l'accordo cromatico fra le immagini riportate); dove queste ultime (le armi progettuali) sono anche espressione di una presa di posizione culturale che parte dalla scelta editoriale del soggetto e dalla selezione del materiale atto a raccontarlo. Un esempio viene proprio dalla suddivisione in categorie di questo

continua a pag 8

Sources, projects, images

by Carlo Branzaglia

The purpose of sources

A book like this, maybe, doesn't need a critical contribution that analyzes its contents: a fascinated and fascinating journey through a series of well selected images. But this will allow us to evaluate the real importance of these source books for a visual culture, as we might define it. The word 'source book' might sound a little generic, since it can be used for a wide range of books already forming a specific editorial gender, composed by different kind of books with different purposes: to inspire, to update, or even to be used by others. By these terms, source books (of images) we mean different kinds of volumes : for example annals (as an updating tool), or titles that include images with common themes (such as postcards or sales displays, as inspirational tools), or catalogues of decorations or even of 'clip art', now confined in computer files (aiming for a recycling use, with or without manipulation, of the original images).

These different editorial products, with their different purposes, in any case, have been created because of the idea that an image is not a finished product that can be used or manipulated for many reasons : to understand the modern trends surrounding us, to steal the basic formal ingredients, or to manipulate well known images.

All activities which are needed by people working in a visual and graphic business. This synchronical vision describes perfectly, in a short and simple way, an aspect of the present market situation, a parallel market which involves an international community of graphic designers, ilustrators, copy-writers, but even stylists and product designers. On the other hand, if we want to have fun with a diachronic analysis, we should realize that the first examples of this particular editorial product date back to the very famous 'The Grammar of Ornament' by Owen Jones, published in London in 1856.

This reminds us that the problem of sources is inside the nature of this project: also the book by Jones is part of the discussion (the dates prove it) which brought to the developement (first of all in Great Britain) of the actual culture of graphic design, thanks to the fertile soil of the newborn Universal Expositions, in which the products are displayed (and Jones himself was a supervisor for the first one, in London in 1851), thanks to the creation of decorative arts museums (Victoria and Albert Museum opened in 1852), thanks even to the debate (in Parliament) about the education on this project. Waiting for a formal synthesis of Arts and Crafts.

The visual text

You don't have to underestimate this world: its pragmatic utility not only involves the pure knowledge but also its practical side, to know something and to know how to do it. Perhaps Owen Jones understood this problem in advance: he understood the need of giving unfinished products to the creators of 'complex' images of those days, a group of professionals on the way of developping an art. The echo of the comprehension of the problem, in a very different context, of course, and actually dominated by the need of an offer 'just in time' (for example the books rapidly released about web design), can be found in the quality of books like the one we are introducing here. We have to point out that the idea of using an editor, requires an understanding, an overall view, a magnifying glass through which the material, which has been collected, is organized.

It isn't an absolute novelty that a book of images shows the work of an editor behind the organisation of its contents, but we haven't taken a moment, yet, to think of two elements. The first is the particularity of the form of a book made of images, and its ability to give information in a way which is completely different from the structure of a book made of words. The second is the cultural peculiarity of a text generated by a project editor (such as Cristiana Valentini and Gabriele Fantuzzi, hidden behind the name of their agency Delicatessen in charge of the creation of this work), using the word text to remind that any form of communication (even the visual one) represents a text to be understood.

Of course these two elements are connected. Well, to be true, the solution has been given by Alber Steiner in his writings (after World War II), when he was talking about the 'graphic editor', pointing out (well in advance) the need of handling the information by the one in charge of the layout of the page (its 'mise-en-scène'). As a result of that idea, there is 'Il Politecnico' , the magazine directed by Ello Vittorini, where the importance of the graphic aspect is cultural and political at the same time.

In the quality of graphic design, we recognize its ability to transfer information in the relationship between text and image; and when the iconographic structure gets big (magazines, books, web sites), a good selection and its layout in a space-time relationship are a way of communication. How many times have we said, about the best magazines of images, that the pictures were able to speak for themselves, with words as mere supporting elements, although useful?

Knowing and doing

The main feature of this book is that, made by designers for other designers, it uses items very commonly used by the community of graphic designers. Technical means (the formats, the text, the quality of reproductions) and project plans (the cage, the layout, the colour harmony among the images), and these plans are also the result of a precise cultural point

continue pag 9

emma.mori *koakuma baby , artist's collection, Illustrator 9.0*

Dunque, volendo commentare un volume come questo, forse la formula migliore potrebbe non essere una classica introduzione, come questa; ma una serie di chiose, di note a margine, di appunti che costruiscano dapprima un background iconologico, poi annotino le sue ripercussioni formali nelle scelte stilistiche. Magari la prossima volta ci si può provare... Un background iconologico: il vecchio PANOFSKY è sempre utile, con le sue definizioni: con iconologia lui intendeva quell'insieme di questioni culturali (sociali, politiche, religiose...) che fungono da quadro di riferimento esplicativo nei confronti delle opere. Beh, noi (occidentali in genere) dovremmo davvero prenderci la briga di costruire un quadro iconologico della produzione giapponese di immagini, perché fatichiamo a individuare, comprendere e spiegare la quantità di stimoli visuali provenienti dall'Estremo Oriente.

Iconologie

Procediamo per schizzi, per appunti, per note: non ci possiamo permettere un quadro organico. Tanto per divertirci, potremmo intanto affermare che la prima forma di immaginario stilistico non realista, basato su criteri figurativi radicalmente nuovi, appare in occidente quando un famoso gallerista, BING, socio peraltro del signor Tiffany, incomincia a importare a Parigi stampe giapponesi, quelle famose cui si ispireranno (siamo a fine Ottocento) TOULOUSE-LAUTREC e compagnia bella (come narra la leggenda). Tutto il simbolismo dialoga con ascendenze orientali (lontane o medie che siano): il cartellonista MUCHA nacque nell'attuale Repubblica Ceca, nella Wiener Werkstatte è evidentissimo l'influsso dell'adiacente Impero Ottomano... Ma i gironi nostri sono più intriganti. Un'altra nota: il Giappone è innanzitutto un grande produttore di hardware e software per l'informazione; settore al quale sembra siano stati destinati quegli investimenti impossibilitati ad essere finalizzati all'industria bellica dopo la sconfitta nella seconda guerra mondiale. Un progetto politico che andrebbe studiato, a sua volta, tanto sembra essere preciso. I conti sono presto fatti: sappiamo tutti quanta tecnologia esporta questo paese; sappiamo anche che i produttori stessi di tecnologia hanno da una ventina di anni operato un processo di acquisizione dei contenuti (vedi ad es. il gruppo Sony - Sony Music - Columbia Pictures). Sappiamo che le tirature dei quotidiani, a parità di popolazione, sono quasi dieci volte maggiori in Giappone che in Italia. Sappiamo che l'innovazione tecnologica viaggia su ritmi anticipati rispetto a quelli occidentali, trainata da un consumo di hardware e software per l'informazione che comunque non ha uguali. E sappiamo, ancora, che industrie come quella del *cartooning* e del fumetto raggiungono gradi di sofisticazione produttiva inediti: data base di immagini, distribuzione, articolazione del prodotto su video, cinema, videogiochi, merchandising. Quest'ultima nota, fra le altre apparentemente casuali, ci permette di comprendere che il consumo di immagini nella terra del Sol Levante è elevatissimo, e come tale targettizzato e specializzato. Il che significa una fortissima articolazione dei prodotti per fasce d'età (non molto rispettata in Occidente per quanto riguarda il *cartooning*); e il ricorso anche a qualità tecniche per noi inusuali (chiunque stampi per il mercato giapponese lo sa). Significa infine che la tale iperproduzione, ormai chiaramente destinata a un mercato su scala globale, ha bisogno a sua volta di fonti di ispirazione. Ecco la leggenda del giapponese che copia, e l'ironia sulla mania classica del turista estremo orientale di fotografare. Ma il Giappone ha studiato e appreso la nostra cultura figurativa meglio di quanto forse non la conosciamo noi. Basti vedere i loro paperback dedicati alla storia dell'arte occidentale: molto meglio, per qualità di immagini, impaginati, e anche prezzi, di qualunque manuale nostrano. Poi, diciamolo: ci avranno anche copiato, ma sta di fatto che il nostro immaginario è dominato da forme di provenienza estremo orientale: dal fumetto (linee pulite, prospettive vertiginose) al design, alla moda, alla fotografia (quel taglio flashato tipico di parte della cultura *kawaii*).

Morfologie

Abbiamo scomodato Panofsky, lasciamo stare WÖLFFLIN: non inoltriamoci cioè nella selva oscura delle possibili implicazioni della parola stile. Sottolineiamo solo quanto accennato in precedenza, a proposito della divisione del volume in categorie: lo stile si sviluppa da scelte formali (che ovviamente coinvolgono opzioni tecniche) attraverso le quali è possibile individuare un approccio personale (lo stile di un autore), culturale (quello di una corrente) ma anche epocale (una sorta di *Zeitgeist*). Non ci preoccupiamo quindi subito di fare una carrellata autore per autore (modello obsoleto e canonico per le collettive d'arte); ma vediamo quali filiere stilistiche (e innegabilmente semantiche) si possono dipanare. Ancora note a margine, dunque, tratteggiate più che debitamente estese.

volume, che facendo riferimento al settore della moda si muove nel terreno scivoloso della modificazione continua degli immaginari. Così, i termini *stylishly*, *vectorize* e *extravaganza* suddividono gli autori presentati in maniera lieve, come un suggerimento più che come una categoria definitiva; ma rappresentano anche un coacervo di significati che vanno dal piano tecnico a quello formale a quello stilistico, con tutte le connotazioni che quest'ultimo assume sul piano degli immaginari. *Vectorize*, dunque, tanto per fare un esempio, ci ricorda indubbiamente le matrici tecniche della grafica vettoriale; che significano anche una predominanza della linea netta di contorno; e quindi una tendenza alla sintesi figurale, una sua concretezza (cioè costruzione con elementi concreti come ad es. le forme geometriche); e infine quell'immaginario fra Fifties e Sixties (ovviamente abbondantemente remixato), anni nei quali queste scelte morfologiche videro particolare affermazione.

Un'altra volta, una mossa editoriale e progettuale che determina dei percorsi di senso: una attitudine tipica della cultura del progetto. Questo a dire che volumi come questo non vanno valutati solo per il loro contenuto, anche se certo, in un *source book* il contenuto è determinante. Essi vanno anche visti come un progetto culturale, e quindi letti, e interpretati, nelle scelte che stanno a monte: la cernita degli autori, quella delle loro opere, l'accostamento fra gli stessi e fra le stesse, l'importanza data dall'impaginato, a questa immagine o a quella. E' anche vero che molte cose vengono date per scontate, in un ambiente molto acculturato sul piano dell'immagine, come è quello degli autori e dei destinatari di tale volume. Il saper fare spesso porta a nascondere il sapere, proprio perché questo sapere è finalizzato alla pragmatica; il che lo rende ingiustamente secondario sia agli occhi del progettista (tecnico del saper fare) che agli occhi del saggista (esperto nel sapere). Ingiustamente, perché sia l'uno (il progettista) dovrebbe rendersi conto che la sua stessa statura professionale deriva esattamente da questa sorta di autocoscienza, poiché la differenza nel cosa si sa fare deriva da una differenza di metodologia, quindi di sapere strutturato. E l'altro (il saggista) dovrebbe rendersi conto che esistono altri modi di sapere, di eguale intensità e strutturazione, solo di differente finalizzazione.

continua a pag 10

of view originated by the editorial choice of the subject and the material selected to describe it.

An example of this choice comes from the separation of this book by subjects, which, with the world of fashion as a reference, moves on the slippery ground of constant change of imagination. So, the terms 'stylishly', 'vectorize' and 'extravaganza' separates the authors in a light way, acting more like a suggestion than a specific category, but they also represent an accumulation of meanings, going from a technical vision to a formal one to a stylish one, with all the implications concerned in the latter one in everyone's imagination. Vectorize, for example, reminds us, no doubt about it, the technical origins of vectorial graphic technique, meaning also the prevailing of the contour lines, and so a trend towards figure synthesis, its concreteness (for example using concrete elements such as geometrical forms), and, last but not least, the imaginary from the Fifties and the Sixties (abundantly remixed of course), years when this kind of forms were pretty popular and successful. Again, an editorial and design choice that establishes paths of meaning : a typical attitude of the culture of design. This means that volumes such as this don't have to be evaluated only for their content, although the content, being a source book, is very important. They must be seen as a cultural project, and therefore read and evaluated for the choices originally made: the selection of the authors, that of their works, the mix between them, the importance given by the layout to this or to that picture. It is also true that a lot of things are given for granted in an image educated world such as that of the authors and of those for which the book is dedicated. The know-how often leads to forget the pure knowledge, just because this knowledge is finalized to the regular practice, and this keeps it wrongly secondary to the eyes of either the designer (the one who has the know-how) and the essayist (expert in the knowledge). Wrongly, because one (the designer) should relize that his own professional stature comes exactly from this kind of self-esteem, because the difference in the know-how comes from a difference in the method, which means a knowledge with a structure, and the other (the essayist) should realize that there are other ways of knowledge, of equal intensity and structure, with just a different finalization.

However, having to comment a book like this one, maybe the best formula wouldn't be a classical one, such as this, but maybe a series of notes, glosses, sketches which should first create an iconological background, and then should make a point of its formal repercussions in the style choices. Maybe we can try next time...

An iconological background: the old Panofsky is always useful, with his definitions. With iconology he meant the group of cultural matters (social, political, religious...) which forms a background reference to explain the works of art. Well, we (Westerners in general) should take our time to build an iconological picture of the Japanese production of images, since we hardly spot, understand and explain the quantity of visual stimulations coming from the Far East.

ryutaro **odagiri**
new japan's play
artist's collection
Illustrator 9.0

Iconologies

Let's proceed by drafts, by notes, by glosses : we cannot afford to see the whole picture. Just for fun, we could say that the first form of a new imaginary style not connected to reality, based on completely new design ideas, appears in the western world when a famous art-gallery owner, Bing, also partner of Mr. Tiffany, starts to bring into Paris some Japanese prints, the famous ones which will inspire (we are at the end of 19th century) Toulouse-Lautrec and all the others (as the legend tells).

The whole symbolism flirts with eastern elements (either middle - or far -): the poster designer Mucha was born in the Czech Republic, in the Wiener Werkstatte it is quite obvious the influence of the Ottoman Empire...

But our times are even more intriguing. Another note: Japan is first of all a great producer of hardware and software for communication; this is a type of business towards which a lot of investments go, since Japanese were not allowed to invest in war industry after World War II. This is a political project that should be analyzed, since it seems being planned with precision. Just consider this : we know how much technolgy that country exports worldwide; we also know that the producers of this technology have started in the last twenty years a process of acquisition of contents (for example Sony group - Sony Music- Columbia Pictures). We know that press sales are almost ten times bigger in Japan than in Italy. We know that technological innovation runs at a faster pace than in the Western world, thanks to a massive demand of hardware and software with no equals in the world. And we also know that industries like cartooning and comics reach an incredible level of sofisticated production: data bases of images, distribution, variety of products on video, cinemas, video games and merchandising.

This last note, among the others, allows us to understand that the consumption of images in Japan is very strong , and therefore highly specific for the different targets. This means a wide range of products by age groups (not well respected in the West in the world of cartooning), it also means technical quality expectations unknown to us (very well known to whomever prints for the Japanese market). It means, after all, that this iperproduction, which is made for a global market, also requires some sort of inspiration sources. And here comes the legend of the Japanese who copies, and the jokes about the mania of far-eastern tourists to take pictures. But Japan studied and understood our figurative culture much better than us. Just take a look at their paperbacks dedicated to the history of western arts: much better, as per quality of images, layouts, and even prices, than any of our western manual. Then, let's say it: maybe they have copied us, but our imaginary is dominated by forms of far-eastern origins. Starting from comics (clean contour lines, vertiginous perspectives), to design elements, to fashion, to photography (that flashlight cut, typical of kawaii traditions).

Morphologies

We have disturbed Panofsky, so let's leave Wölfflin alone: we won't get into the deep dark wood of the possible implications of the word 'style'. Let's just explain what we briefly mentioned before, about the categories into which the volume is divided: the style is made by formal choices (involving, of course, technical options) through which it is possible to recognize an approach which is personal (the style of an author), cultural (the style of a trend), but even by epochs (a sort of Zeitgeist).

continue pag 11

hiroshi fujii *apartment. NHK tv. Illustrator & Photoshop*

Una prima questione riguarda l'illustrazione.

Una prima questione riguarda l'illustrazione. Disciplina appartenente indubbiamente al *corpus* della progettazione, del design, in questo stesso *corpus* è quella che più indulge verso elementi fenomenici evidenti, quella nella quale cioè il tratto, lo stile dell'autore è evidente, e deve esserlo. Ma un'altra volta tale stile si traduce (come nel product, graphic e interior design) in uno stile progettuale che propone la soluzione (in questo caso figurativa) a problemi di visualizzazione. E' dunque uno stile che rimane senz'altro riconoscibile, ma che oscilla a seconda della problematica proposta; e che, come per tutte le discipline progettuali, attraverso la sensibilità dell'autore, la sua capacità di leggere tra le righe della cultura di una società, dà forma a ciò che è latente.

Poi, siamo nel campo dell'illustrazione di moda, settore nel quale le oscillazioni si fanno davvero frequenti e sottili. In questo caso è necessario individuare delle priorità espressive, ben rese se vogliamo proprio dal titolo di un'altra delle categorie che organizzano il materiale di questo volume: *stilyshly*. Che potremo tradurre con il gergale "stiloso", ad indicare una delle mosse fondamentali del sistema della moda, la distinzione (non trasgressiva) rispetto al gruppo, oggi arrivata a sottigliezze stilistiche indicibili in un mondo dominato dall'iperscelta di oggetti/comportamenti. C'è un tono *understatement* in questo termine, così come c'è nelle immagini raccolte in questo volume: una ricerca della finezza stilizzata nella forma, e della precisione nel dettaglio. Ma questo tono è un segnale, casomai ce ne fosse bisogno, della inesistenza di un sistema della moda basato esclusivamente su *plus* simbolici. Inutile ricordare che in inglese lo stilista è un fashion designer, non un'artista prestato ai vestiti. Il fatto che gli autori siano quasi tutti giovani ci porta a considerare questa selezione come una rappresentazione fresca ed *up-to-date* dello stato dell'arte; e anche a stimolare future indagini, speriamo, sulla evidente maturità professionale degli autori raccolti. Mentre un altro dato comune, l'utilizzo di tecniche informatiche, ci porta a una annotazione: ricordiamoci che nella comunicazione (visiva, nel caso particolare) la nostra percezione regna; ed essa non fa differenza fra un acquerello "vero" ed uno mimato da un software informatico, così come non faceva differenza fra finti e veri marmi nelle chiese (se non da vicino...). La logica dell'effetto fenomenico, legato alle tecniche e ai materiali, è fondante: può interessare all'illustratore sapere quali mirabilie escano da un programma come *Illustrator* (così come interessa sapere quali vengano invece da una matita). Ma per il fruitore se quell'*Illustrator* dà l'effetto di un pastello a cera, vale quanto un pastello a cera.

Matrici

Ovvio inoltre che dobbiamo fare i conti con le matrici stilistiche giapponesi. Qui forse troviamo delle sorprese gustose, come peraltro annotato nella prefazione di DELICATESSEN: abituati a pensare al cartooning giapponese, ci saremmo aspettati più occhioni a mandorla e tratti a pennino, che ci sono, per carità, in NAGAO, SOUZEN, OTA, WAKABA, ma anche in chiave fortemente ironica, come è evidentissimo in EMMA, RINGIRL, SHIMOTASHIRO. In realtà è un'altra volta un deficit culturale: è vero che questi sono toni dominanti in *manga* e *anime*, ma molto evidenti soprattutto nella produzione infantile/primo adolescenziale importata nel nostro paese (e in occidente in genere); più sfumata (non assente, per carità) in segmenti più adulti di cui comunque abbiamo avuto sentore, vedi la spettacolare serie tv *Evangelion*, trasmessa da MTV, o pellicole cinematografiche come *Akira*, *Ghost in the Shell*, *Metropolis*.

Ma è ovvio che qui i toni sono incredibilmente più variegati, con recuperi indubbi anche nei confronti della tradizione illustrativa giapponese, talora debitamente citati se non altro a livello iconografico (da NAGAO, UESUGI, TAMIYA, KONO, ad esempio).

Soprattutto, ci sembra però siano evidentemente figlie della cultura figurativa giapponese le due matrici che accomunano tutti gli autori presentati, nella grande varietà di toni e nella peculiarità dei singoli: la bidimensionalità e il decorativismo. La bidimensionalità si risolve non solo nelle figure assolutamente stilizzate, piatte; ma soprattutto nella resa di uno spazio che si ribalta, quasi, verso il lettore, erede di una prospettiva (quella tradizionale di UTAMARO per intenderci sommariamente) che non ha le stesse regole della nostra, e che negli stessi *manga* determina montaggi dell'immagine inconsueti, per la nostra cultura. Ad esempio MACCOSI (che ci ricorda come anche Matisse avesse a suo tempo guardato al Giappone), YOSHIOKA (che ci gioca, con le linee della prospettiva), SOUZEN (che mette in crisi il ruolo dello sfondo). Con una eccezione formidabile e significativa: HIROSHI FUJII, che prende di petto il problema contrapponendo sagome concrete e appena costruite con sfumature di tonalità, a sfondi ricavati da immagini fotografiche. Il decorativismo è presente nella raffinatezza delle arti e delle arti applicate della tradizione giapponese: non a caso esso riappare massicciamente in Europa a fine Ottocento. Un decorativismo che dialoga con lo spazio riducendolo (vedi sopra) a sua volta a due dimensioni: in TAMIYA, YUGE, EMMA, SHIMOTASHIRO, UMEZAWA (che recupera dalla sua una dimensione popolare molto peculiare, all'apparenza est europea)

Navigazioni

Ci sembra però arguto, e significativo, l'appunto finale di DELICATESSEN: quelle tavole nelle quali *Italy meets Japan* ci raccontano con lo stile di Delicatessen che la varietà di input stilistici presenti negli autori raccolti può effettivamente far sì che l'Italia incontri il Giappone. Visto che il contrario (che il Giappone incontri l'Italia) è evidentemente già avvenuto. Inutile soffermarsi sulla presenza di toni provenienti dall'illustrazione di moda degli anni Cinquanta, soprattutto francese: UESUGI (con straordinarie inquadrature fumettistico/cinematografiche), MACCOSI, HASEGAWA, YOSHIOKA, TAKAJAMA (eccezionale il mix fra collage e tratto schizzato). Il *mood* lounge che avvolge oggi il pianeta non sfugge ai nostri: già latente in parte degli autori appena citati, trionfa nel suo splendore vettorializzato nell'oscillazione fra cromie anni Cinquanta e Sessanta in KONO, SHIMOTASHIRO, RINGIRL (che ci mette dei bei toni cinetico/psichedelici). Ancora "vettoriali", ma in versione più legata al *web cartooning* di provenienza underground occidentale, sono MAEDA, ODAGIRI e TANIGUCHI. I toni *street*, a livello iconografico, entrano nei puppet di HASEBE (con un finto naif delizioso), e dominano i disegni di WAKABA, che richiama però la linea cosiddetta espressionista del *comics* occidentale (quella Milton Caniff - Hugo Pratt), le cui estreme conseguenze potrebbero essere tratte da MINETA, alcune immagini della quale richiamano anche l'ultimo Mattotti. E questa è solo una serie di appunti a margine, robusta, come robuste erano d'altronde, nel loro insieme, le glosse apposte dagli amanuensi. Un piccolo percorso di navigazione che assume forma testuale ma che forse, scusate la ripetizione, dovrebbe assumere una paratestuale, o ipertestuale addirittura. Una formula che permetterebbe di navigare compiutamente (liberamente?) fra le suggestioni, editoriali, progettuali, stilistiche che "mondofragile" propone.

carlo branzaglia

風水

We won't bother to examine the book author by author (which is a common and obsolete way to describe a collective art exhibition), but we will see which style paths (even semantics) we will be able to follow. Again, a lot of glosses and notes will appear every now and then to explain a little more, although not too deeply . The first question will concern the illustration. An art which is part of the core of design, it is actually the art that shows the real style of the author, as it should be. But, at times, the same style could be (as in product, graphic and interior design) a design style that gives a solution (graphically, in this case) to a visual problem. It is, anyway, a style that remains recognizable after all, but that can vary according to the different needs, and it goes , as in all design arts, through the sensitivity of the author, his ability to read between the lines of the culture of a society, and gives form to what is evident.

Then, we are in the field of fashion illustration, a field where changes and variations are really frequent and fine. In this case it is necessary to find the expressive priorities, which are well indicated by the title of another category of this book : stylishly. Almost imposible to translate in Italian, it indicates one of the most important aspects of fashion world, the distinction (without shocking) from the masses, which is created, today, by many fine stylish differences in a world which is dominated by the huge freedom of choice (of objects and behaviours). There is an understatement tone in this term, as there is one in the images presented in this volume: a research of the finesse in the style, and in the precision in the detail. But this tone is a signal, in case we needed one, of the non-existence of a fashion system created upon symbolic pluses. It is not neccessary to point out that in English a stylist is a fashion designer, not an artist dedicated to make clothes.

The fact that almost all the authors are young , leads us to consider this selection as a fresh and up-to-date representation of the state of the art, and also to stimulate future analysis, hopefully, about the future developpements of the authors concerned in this book. While another common element, the use of informatic techniques, brings us another thought: let's remember that in communication (visual, in this case) our perception reigns; it won't make any difference between a real watercolour paint and one 'created' by a computer software, as it didn't make any difference between real marbles and fake ones in the old churches (or at least only after a very close examination). Logically speaking, it is important for designers and illustrators to see which wonderful things can come out of an Illustrator pogrmmme, but for the common observer, if that Illustrator programmme gives the idea of a wax pastel, it has the same value of a wax pastel.

Foundations

It is quite obvious, of course, that we have to evaluate the foundations of the Japanese style. Here maybe we will find more interesting surprises, as already pointed out in the introduction by Delicatessen: because of the way we are used to think of Japanese cartooning, we would expect more almond-eyed characters and ink pen drawings,

that are included of course, by Nagao, Souzen, Ota, Wakaba, but also in a very ironical way, as it is obvious in Emma, Ringirl, Shimotashiro. Actually it is another case of cultural deficit: it is true that these are the main tones in manga and anime, but mostly very clear in the production for infantile/early teen markets imported in our continent, and more subtle (not absent, of course) in more adult products, that we have seen, anyway, like the spectacular tv series of Evangelion, shown by MTV, or movies like Akira, Ghost in the Shell, and Metropolis. But it is obvious that the tones here are incredibly more variegated, using evident elements from the illustrative Japanese tradition, at times clearly stated, at least at an iconographical level (by Nagao, Uesugi, Tamiya, Kono, for example).

Mainly, we think that there are two foundations which are a common thread for all the authors presented, even in the great variety of tones and in the peculiarities of each and everyone of them: the bidemensional structure and the decorations.

The bidemansional structure is not only in the absolutely stylized and flat figures, but mainly in a space that goes basically towards the reader, originating from a traditional perspective (that of Utamaro, for example) that has different rules from ours, and that, in the manga drawings, involve editings of images which are quite unusual, at least for our culture. Maccosi, for instance, who reminds us how Matisse, too, had once looked at Japan; Yoshioka, who plays with the lines of perspective; Souzen, who questions the role of background images. With an incredible and meaningful exception: Hiroshi Fujii, who confronts the problem by counterpoising concrete figures, drawned lightly and with shades of tone, against backgrounds taken from photo images. The decorations are evident in the fine arts of the Japanese tradition: it is not accidental that they appear so extensively in Europe (at the same time of the applied arts) at the end of 19th Century. The decorative art that talks to the space and reduces it (as seen above) to a bidimensional form : in Tamyia, Yuge, Emma, Shimotashiro, Umezawa (who uses a popular dimension which is very peculiar, apparently east-european).

Navigations

The final note of Delicatessen seems to us quite clever and meaningful: the pictures in the 'Italy meets Japan' section tell us, with the style of Delicatessen, that the variety of stylish inputs, which are evident in this collection, can actually help Italy meeting Japan. As it is quite obvious that the contrary (Japan meeting Italy) has already happened. There is no point talking about the tones coming from the fashion illustrations of the Fifties, mainly French (but also Italian): Uesugi, with extraordinary comic/cinema oriented framings, Maccosi, Hasegawa, Yoshioka, Takajama (with a superb mix between collage and ink strokes). The mood lounge that surrounds our planet is pretty clear to these authors: it is pretty evident in some of the authors already cited, but it explodes in his vectorial splendor in the oscillation between shades of colours of the Fifties and the Sixties in Kono, Shimotashiro, Ringirl (who adds some kinetic/psychedelic colours, as well). Also 'vectorial', but in a way which is more related to the web cartooning of Western underground origin, are Maeda, Odagiri and Taniguchi. The street tones, iconographically speaking, are part of the puppets of Hasebe (with a nice fake naif tone), and dominate the drawings of Wakaba, who, actually, reminds the so said expressionist line of the western comics (that of Milton Caniff and Hugo Pratt), whose extreme consequences could be found in Mineta, some pictures of whom recall even the latest Mattotti.

And this is just a series of notes, robust, as robust were, in a way, the glosses that the amanuensis friars wrote. A little navigation journey in a textual form which should be, perhaps, and excuse the repetition, in a paratextual one, or even ipertextual. A formula that would allow us to navigate completely (freely?) among the editorial, design and stylistic ideas that this volume undoubtly suggests.

carlo branzaglia

tadahiro **uesugi** tokyo

this page
untitled
paperback book
cover art
Adobe Photoshop

opposite
untitled
magazine cover art
Adobe Photoshop

above
untitled
magazine cover art
Adobe Photoshop and watercolor

opposite above
untitled
magazine cover art
Adobe Photoshop and watercolor

opposite below
untitled
artist's collection
Adobe Photoshop

untitled
artist's collection
Adobe Photoshop and watercolor

this page
untitled
Art for Jill Stuart
Adobe Photoshop

opposite
untitled
Illustration for japanese magazine
Adobe Photoshop

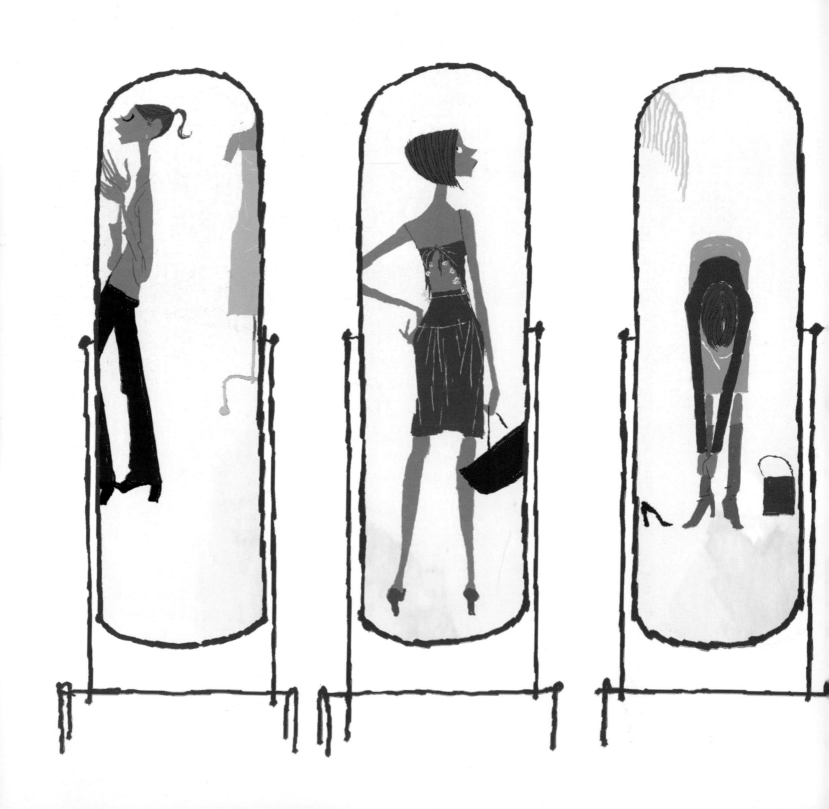

this page
untitled
Illustration for japanese interior shop catalog
Adobe Photoshop

opposite
untitled
Illustration for japanese magazine
Adobe Photoshop

this page
Cover art for japanese
company magazine
Adobe Photoshop

opposite
untitled
artist's collection
Adobe Photoshop

above
untitled
artist's collection
Adobe Photoshop

opposite
Art for Jill Stuart
Adobe Photoshop

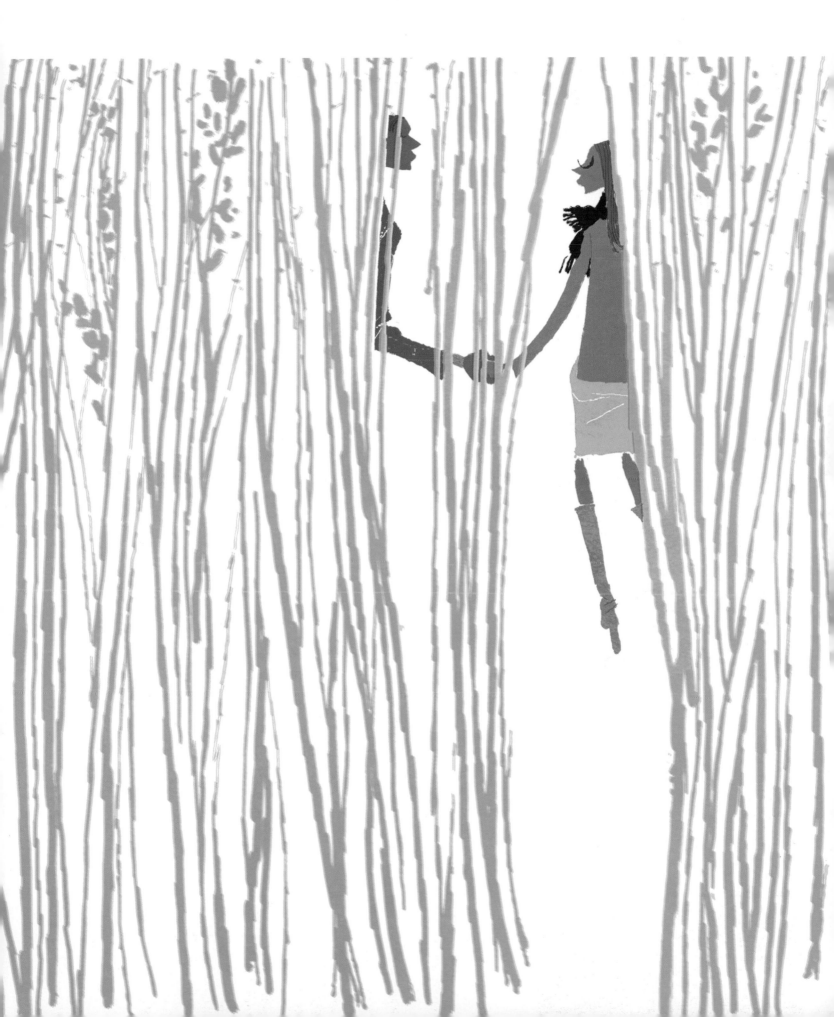

above
untitled
Illustration for japanese magazine
Adobe Photoshop

right
untitled
paperback book cover art
(HARLEQUIN ROMANCE japanese edition)
Adobe Photoshop

opposite
untitled
paperback book cover art
(HARLEQUIN ROMANCE japanese edition)
Adobe Photoshop

sai **tamiya** tokyo

this page
Natsuko
artist's collection
Painter, Photoshop

opposite
Hitomi
artist's collection
Painter, Photoshop

this page above right
Electric fan
Raining Pleasure "Flood"/
CD jacket
(MINOS-EIM/Greece)
Painter, Photoshop

this page above left
Aoi
artist's collection
Painter, Photoshop

this page below
Bathing time
artist's collection
Painter, Photoshop

opposite
Sleeping beauty
artist's collection
Painter, Photoshop

this page above
Megumi
artist's collection
Painter, Photoshop

this pagebelow left
Hitomi
artist's collection
Painter, Photoshop

this page below
The girl who put up a parasol
Raining Pleasure "Capricorn" CD jacket
(MINOS-EIM/Greece)
Painter, Photoshop

opposite
Giovanni
Raining Pleasure "Fake" CD jacket
(MINOS-EIM/Greece)
Painter, Photoshop

this page above left
Haruka "A spring scent"
artist's collection
Painter, Photoshop

this page above right
Sidarezakura
"A drooping cherry tree"
Nihon Keizai Shimbun
(Newspaper)
Painter, Photoshop

this page below
Pears
artist's collection
Painter, Photoshop

opposite
Ryouhu
"Refreshing breeze"
Nihon Keizai Shimbun
(Newspaper)
Painter, Photoshop

hitomi **nagao**

kobe

this page above left
horoscope girl
"MISTY" magazine
adobe Illustrator

this page above right
fluffly
artist's collection
ink, pen, Photoshop

this page below
jeans
artist's collection
ink, pen, Photoshop

opposite
untitled
artist's collection
ink, pen, Photoshop

right
girltalk 1 + 2
artist's collection
ink, pen, Photoshop

above
street 2
artist's collection
ink, pen, Photoshop

right
untitled
artist's collection
ink, pen, Photoshop

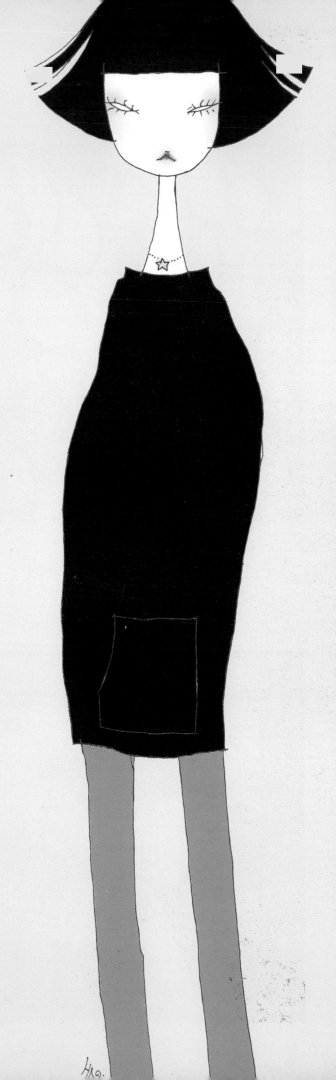

top
clover
artist's collection
ink, pen, Photoshop

left
wisteria
artist's collection
ink, pen, Photoshop

below
umbrera pine
artist's collection
ink, pen, Photoshop

above left
azarea
artist's collection
ink, pen, Photoshop

below left
yosino cherry
artist's collection
ink, pen, Photoshop

below
poppy
artist's collection
ink, pen, Photoshop

holly
artist's collection
ink, pen, Photoshop

lilie
artist's collection
ink, pen, Photoshop

left
kamuro
artist's collection
ink, pen, Photoshop

below
kamuro 2
artist's collection
ink, pen, Photoshop

aries

cancer

aquarius

pisces

scorpio

gemini

sagittarius

virgo

taurus

libra

leo

capricorn

horoscopes
"MISTY" magazine
adobe illustrator

Scorpio

Taurus

Aquarius

Aries

Gemini

Libra

Virgo

Pisces

Cancer

Leo

Sagittarius

Capricorn

horoscopes
"MISTY" magazine
adobe illustrator

maccosi yokohama

this page
bedroom
artist's collection
Adobe Photoshop

opposite
futari
artist's collection
Adobe Photoshop

welcome !
to maccosi's room.

this page above left
namida
artist's collection
Adobe Photoshop

this page below left
room 19
artist's collection
Adobe Photoshop

this page above right
blue
artist's collection
Adobe Photoshop

this page below right
shower
artist's collection
Adobe Photoshop

opposite
sunbath
artist's collection
Adobe Photoshop

this page above left
women
Adobe Photoshop

this page below left
room 25
artist's collection
Adobe Photoshop

this page above right
tea break!
artist's collection
Adobe Photoshop

this page below right
teddy bear
artist's collection
Adobe Photoshop

opposite
friends
artist's collection
Adobe Photoshop

this page
Rosy
Mikimoto cosmetics
Ink, Adobe Photoshop

opposite above left
Je m'appelle...
Matsuya Ginza-Department store
Pencil, Adobe Photoshop

opposite above right
Attends-moi la
Matsuya Ginza-Department store
Pencil, Adobe Photoshop

opposite below left
Vous allez bien?
Matsuya Ginza-Department store
Pencil, Adobe Photoshop

opposite below right
Ca me plait
Matsuya Ginza-Department store
Pencil, Adobe Photoshop

naomi **yuge** osaka

above left
On va quelque part?
Mikimoto cosmetics
Ink, Adobe Photoshop

above right
Bonne journee
Matsuya Ginza-Department store
Pencil, Adobe Photoshop

below left
Male fate
JJ MAGAZINE
Ink, Adobe Photoshop

below right
The woman wearing the hat
artist's collection
Pencil, Adobe Photoshop

above left
long talk
artist's collection
Acrylics paint

above right
Fickleness girl
artist's collection
Acrylics paint

below right
what?
artist's collection
Acrylics paint

below left
Janis
artist's collection
Acrylics paint

hiroko **hasegawa** tokyo

this page
untitled
artist's collection
watercolor

opposite
chaise
artist's collection
watercolor

this page above
untitled
artist's collection
watercolor

this page below left
untitled
artist's collection
watercolor

this page below
untitled
artist's collection
watercolor

opposite
untitled
artist's collection
watercolor

this page above left
sofa
artist's collection
watercolor

opposite
cooking
artist's collection
watercolor

this page above left
untitled
artist's collection
watercolor

this page above right
untitled
artist's collection
watercolor

this page below left
cafe
artist's collection
watercolor

this page below right
table
artist's collection
watercolor

opposite
untitled
artist's collection
watercolor

this page above
untitled
artist's collection
watercolor

this page below left
untitled
artist's collection
watercolor

this page below right
attendre
artist's collection
watercolor

opposite
untitled
artist's collection
watercolor

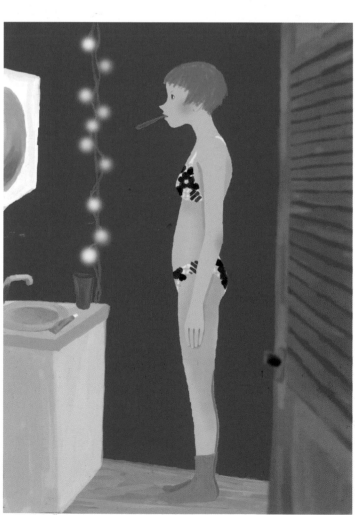

this page above
sweet wedding
artist's collection
Adobe Photoshop

this page below
dog line
artist's collection
Adobe Photoshop

opposite
girl is librarian
artist's collection
Adobe Photoshop

yuko **yoshioka** tokyo

this page
spaghetti&cat
artist's collection
Adobe Photoshop

opposite
rendezvous
artist's collection
Adobe Photoshop

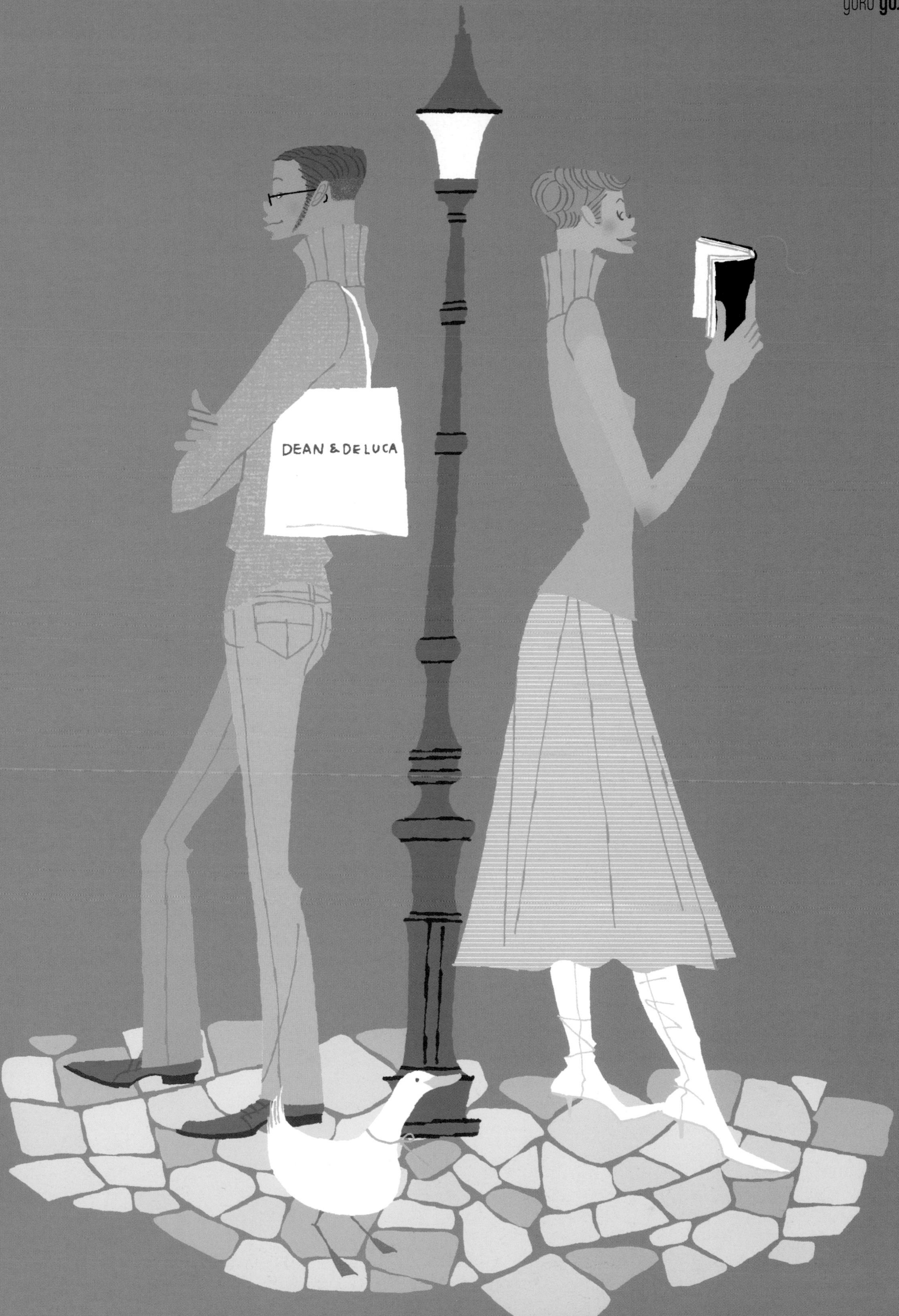
DEAN & DELUCA

this page
nest hairstyle
artist's collection
Adobe Photoshop

opposite
the big bowl bowling
artist's collection
Adobe Photoshop

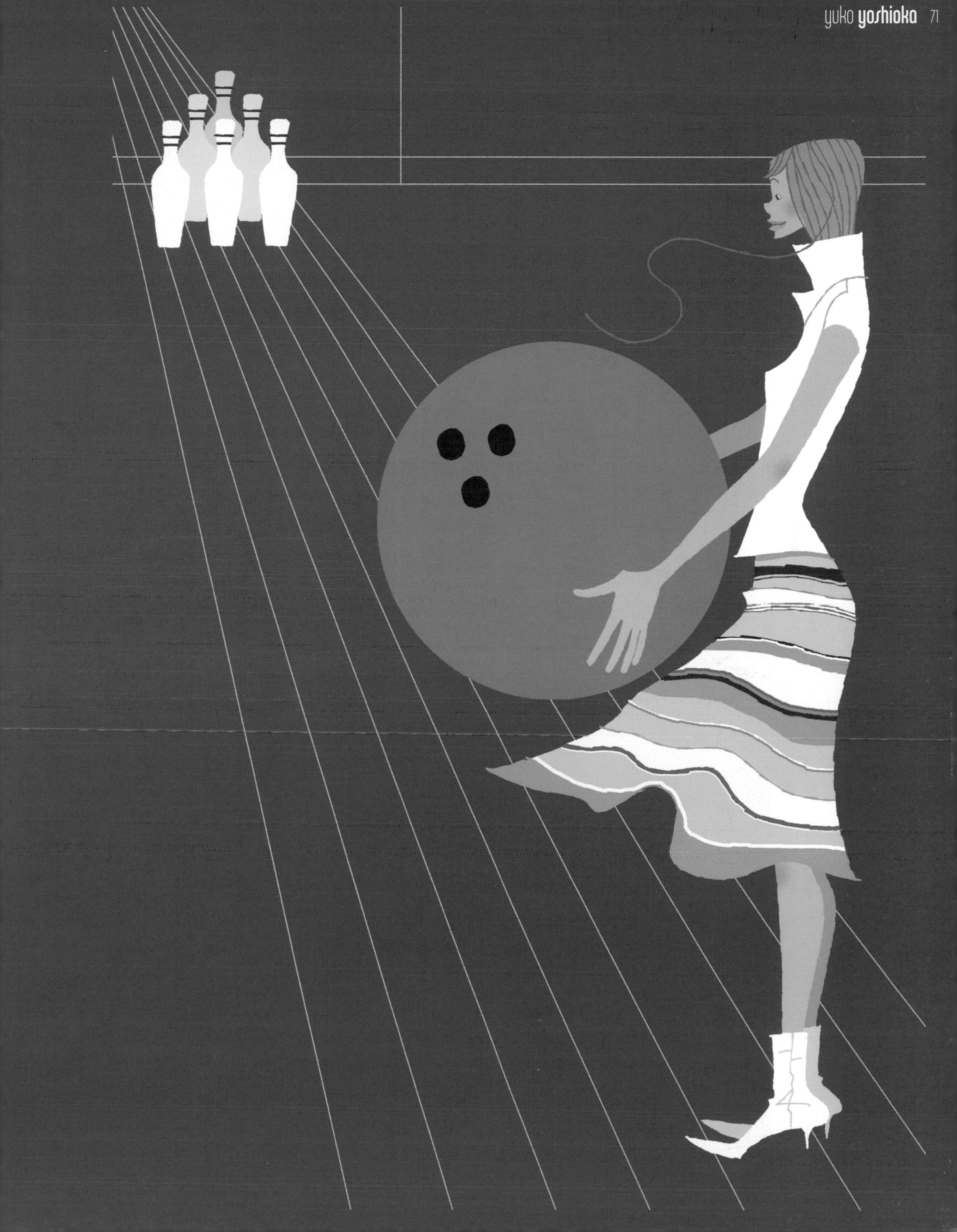

1 janvier

1	2	3	4	5
6	7	8	9	10	11	12
13	14	15	16	17	18	19
20	21	22	23	24	25	26
27	28	29	30	31

2 fèvrier

					1	2
3	4	5	6	7	8	9
10	11	12	13	14	15	16
17	18	19	20	21	22	23
24	25	26	27	28

3 mars

					1	2
4	5	6	7	8	9
11	12	13	14	15	16
18	19	20		22	23
25	26	27	28	29	30

this page + next three
calendar
artist's collection
Adobe Photoshop

4 avril

1	2	3	4	5	6
7	8	9	10	11	12	13
14	15	16	17	18	19	20
21	22	23	24	25	26	27
28	29	30				

5 mai

		1	2	3	4
5	6	7	8	9	10	11
12	13	14	15	16	17	18
19	20	21	22	23	24	25
26	27	28	29	30	31	

hole in one !?

6 juin

						1
2	3	4	5	6	7	8
9	10	11	12	13	14	15
16	17	18	19	20	21	22
23	24	25	26	27	28	29
30						

7 juillet

1	2	3	4	5	6
8	9	10	11	12	13
15	16	17	18	19	20
22	23	24	25	26	27
28	29	30	31		

wao!

8 aout

			1	2	3	
4	5	6	7	8	9	10
11	12	13	14	15	16	17
18	19	20	21	22	23	24
25	26	27	28	29	30	31

9 septembre

1	2	3	4	5	6	7
8	9	10	11	12	13	14
15	16	17	18	19	20	21
22	23	24	25	26	27	28
29	30					

10 octobre

	1	2	3	4	5
6	7	8	9	10	11	12
13	14	15	16	17	18	19
20	21	22	23	24	25	26
27	28	29	30	31

11 novembre

	1	2	3	4	5
6	7	8	9	10	11	12
13	14	15	16	17	18	19
20	21	22	23	24	25	26
27	28	29	30	31

12 dècembre

1	2	3	4	5	6	7
8	9	10	11	12	13	14
15	16	17	18	19	20	21
22	23	24	25	26	27	28
29	30	31

yuka **maeda** osaka-city

this page
meditation
artist's collection
adobe illustrator

opposite
weekend shopping
artist's collection
adobe illustrator

YUKA MAEDA ILLUSTRATION
FLAVOR GIRLS

YUKA MAEDA ILLUSTRATION
FLAVOR GIRLS

this page
party meets
artist's collection
adobe illustrator

opposite
colored carp
artist's collection
adobe illustrator

YUKA MAEDA ILLUSTRATION
FLAVOR BOYS

this page
ballerina
artist's collection
adobe illustrator

opposite
fragile
artist's collection
adobe illustrator

YUKA MAEDA ILLUSTRATION
FLAVOR GIRLS

this page
rainy sunday
artist's collection
adobe illustrator

opposite
delicious
artist's collection
adobe illustrator

emma.mori tokyo

this page above left
tasting
artist's collection
Adobe Illustrator

this page above right
breakfast
artist's collection
Adobe Illustrator

this page below
siesta
artist's collection
Adobe Illustrator

opposite
imagination
artist's collection
Adobe Illustrator

this page above left
clubber
artist's collection
Adobe Illustrator

this page below left
smokin' girl
artist's collection
Adobe Illustrator

this page above right
happy time
artist's collection
Adobe Illustrator

this page below right
I wanna be your dog
artist's collection
Adobe Illustrator

opposite
rainy girl
artist's collection
Adobe Illustrator

One Love

Two Love

Three Love

Four Love

Five Love

Six Love

Seven Love

Eight Love

Nine Love

Ten Love

Eleven Love

Twelve Love

Thirteen Love

Fake Love

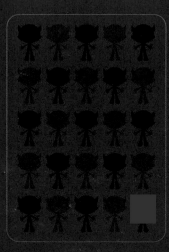

this page
sweet devils
artist collection
Adobe Illustrator

opposite
KO-OKUMA 7 items
artist collection
Adobe Illustrator

KO-AKUMA 7ITEMS

Seven Items which are necessary because it becomes a ko-akuma
but, love is the most important.

long bkack glove

horn headband

devil tail

leather suit

love

Net tights

long boots

Collect these seven items if it is here
because you want to be a ko-akuma.
but, it can't become an actual ko-akuma only by the appearance.
You must get the most important love.

ryutaro **odagiri** tokyo

this page right
a style of japan
artist's collection
Adobe Illustrator

this page below
butterfly girl
artist's collection
Adobe Illustrator

opposite
pleasure of a girl
artist's collection
Adobe Illustrator

this page above
night is safe
artist's collection
Adobe Illustrator

this page right above
cosmetics room
artist's collection
Adobe Illustrator

this page right below
break
artist's collection
Adobe Illustrator

opposite
bicycle girl
artist's collection
Adobe Illustrator

rainfall
artist's collection
Adobe Illustrator

indigo
artist's collection
Adobe Illustrator

opposite
a dreamful of bonsai
artist's collection
Adobe Illustrator

walk
artist's collection
Adobe Illustrator

waiting
artist's collection
Adobe Illustrator

ringirl chiba-ken

*Sutekinakurai
Siroasechattemo
Siinjanai?*

Won't it be pretty nice to fade

The flame not disappearing

The flame wouldn't fade out regardless of wind or rain
The flame wavers eternally.

Will the chick stay a chick if I keep her in a small cage?

Kaze: | nagareru konoha ha
      | marude "koi" wo hakonde iru mitai...

Floating leaves are carrying "LOVE".

Tel.
Bell.
Machiuke.

I'm waiting for your call.

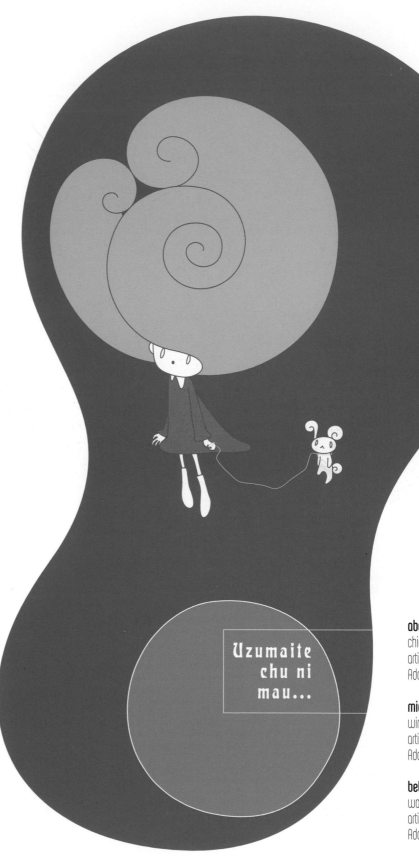

Uzumaite
chu ni
mau...

Bursting, spinning round and floating, drifting into the air.

above left
chick cage
artist's collection
Adobe Illustrator

middle left
wind
artist's collection
Adobe Illustrator

below left
wait
artist's collection
Adobe Illustrator

right
whirlgig
artist's collection
Adobe Illustrator

this page
girl's face
artist's collection
Adobe Illustrator

I came here to see my happy soft ice cream.

heiwa de
douwa na
R G B.

A peaceful RGB colored fairytale filling my mind with rainbow imaginations.

above
ice cream
artist's collection
Adobe Illustrator

below
RGB
artist's collection
Adobe Illustrator

Onaka no naka ha ta-te-shi-ma...

Sparkling mind, vertical striped belly.

Three people are alike me in the world.
My destiny twinkled when I happened to meet are of "ourselves".

above left
inside
artist's collection
Adobe Illustrator

above right
alike
artist's collection
Adobe Illustrator

below left
receiver
artist's collection
Adobe Illustrator

below right
spring hunt
artist's collection
Adobe Illustrator

THIS IS THE RECEIVER.

Phone call with my right hond.
Setting up an antenna - my forefinger.

Spring hunt

Let's go catch some Spring!

Garl

Mimy

Maparon

Kagamimochi
(Round rice cakes offered to the gods at New Year's)

Umarashiki

Yodel

Plain

Mushroom Rabbit

Cake Bear

Autumn and winter style

Wawamu (Telephone dog)

Ringirl

Ringael

Jurin

Boy

Girl

Finger Bunny

Kumo-kumo chan

characters
artist's collection
Adobe Illustrator

chinatsu souzen kagoshima

this page above
inside a fog 1
artist's collection
Adobe Illustrator

this page below
inside a fog 2
artist's collection
Adobe Illustrator

opposite
the spring breeze
artist's collection
Adobe Illustrator

Qu'est-ce qu'il fait beau, aujourd'hui!

this page above left
japan dancing
artist's collection
Adobe Illustrator

this page below left
japan dance
artist's collection
Adobe Illustrator

this page above right
a creature from outer space
artist's collection
Adobe Illustrator

this page below right
the first step
artist's collection
Adobe Illustrator

oppposite
a lantern offering on the water
artist's collection
Adobe Illustrator

Who are you?

monkey!

this page above left
who are you?
artist's collection
Adobe Illustrator

this page above right
a little friend
artist's collection
Adobe Illustrator

this page middle
the banana's ape
artist's collection
Adobe Illustrator

this page below left
the girl take a trip with balloons
artist's collection
Adobe Illustrator

this page below right
the first party
artist's collection
Adobe Illustrator

opposite
let's jump!
artist's collection
Adobe Illustrator

toru **kono** fukuoka-city

above left	**above right**	**below left**	**below right**
yamabuki	ouni	imayou	moegi
artist's collection	artist's collection	artist's collection	artist's collection
Photoshop, Illustrator	Photoshop, Illustrator	Photoshop, Illustrator	Photoshop, Illustrator

above left
uruhanada
artist's collection
Photoshop, Illustrator

above middle
aotake
artist's collection
Photoshop, Illustrator

above right
aomurasaki
artist's collection
Photoshop, Illustrator

below
nadeshiko
artist's collection
Photoshop, Illustrator

yuca **shimotashiro** kagoshima

this page above
mannequin
artist's collection
Adobe Illustrator

this page right
autumn
artist's collection
Adobe Illustrator

opposite
summer
artist's collection
Adobe Illustrator

this page above
beauty salon
artist's collection
Adobe Illustrator

this page below left
make up (repair)
artist's collection
Adobe Illustrator

this page below middle
make up (remove)
artist's collection
Adobe Illustrator

this page below right
washing
artist's collection
Adobe Illustrator

opposite
bathroom
artist's collection
Adobe Illustrator

this page above
a red ballon
artist's collection
Adobe Illustrator

this page below
mommy
artist's collection
Adobe Illustrator

opposite
the little bird
artist's collection
Adobe Illustrator

this page above left
cat's eyes
artist's collection
Adobe Illustrator

this page above right
princess
artist's collection
Adobe Illustrator

this page below left
café
artist's collection
Adobe Illustrator

this page below right
moon
artist's collection
Adobe Illustrator

opposite
modern
artist's collection
Adobe Illustrator

mamiko **hasebe** saitama-ken

this page above left
a florist
artist's collection
oven clay

this page above right
a bride
magazine I WEDDING
oven clay

this page below
LOVE
artist's collection
oven clay

opposite
the hat where rabbits live
artist's collection
oven clay

uyo **takajama** tokyo

this page
smokecar
artist's collection
ink, watercolor,
material, Photoshop

opposite
tabacco
stylus magazine
ink, watercolor,
material, Photoshop

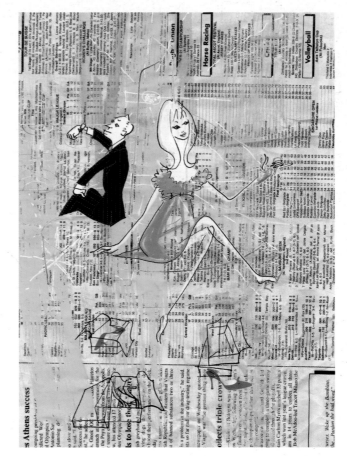

this page above left
sea
artist's collection
ink, watercolor,
material, Photoshop

this page above right
shoeshop
Stylus magazine
ink, watercolor,
material, Photoshop

this page left
bar
artist's collection
ink, watercolor,
material, Photoshop

this page right
tangueray 2
artist's collection
ink, watercolor,
material, Photoshop

opposite
patchwork
artist's collection
ink, watercolor,
material, Photoshop

shiro **taniguchi** tokyo

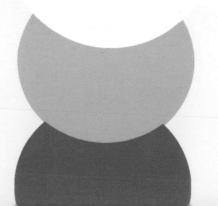

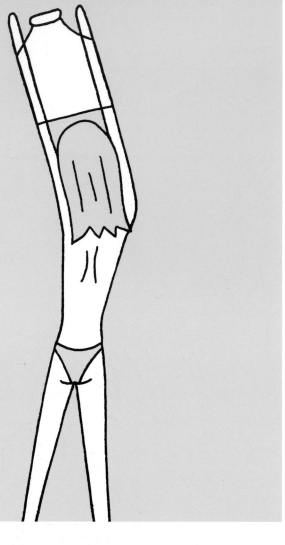

this page above left
lbackstage pass
pen, ink & Photoshop

this page above right
happy hour
pen, ink & Photoshop

this page below left
cut cut cutie
pen, ink & Photoshop

this page above right
one day
pen, ink & Photoshop

opposite
a personal café night mix
pen, ink & Photoshop

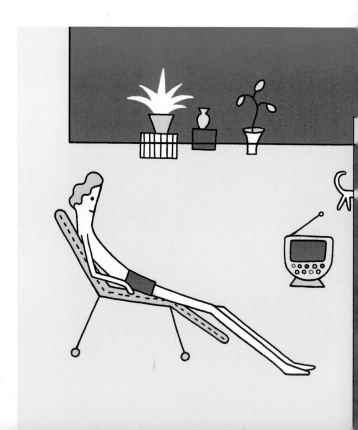

A PERSONAL CAFE NIGHT MIX

above left
seaside picnic
pen, ink & Photoshop

above right
in the art museum
pen, ink & Photoshop

below left
angels help
pen, ink & Photoshop

below right
exercises in free love
pen, ink & Photoshop

above left
miracle + luna
pen, ink & Photoshop

above right
body language
pen, ink & Photoshop

below
new dark ages
pen, ink & Photoshop

NEW DARK AGES

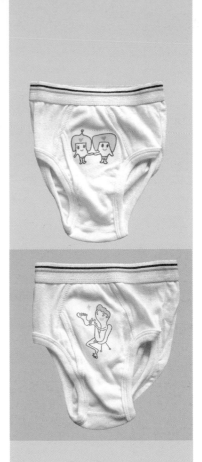

above
brief of children

below
game console

this page right
A favorite bag and a casket
artist's collection
pen and ink
with color markers

this page below
The pattern of a butterfly
artist's collection
pen and ink
with color markers

opposite
summer girl
artist's collection
pen and ink
with color markers

button umezawa tokyo

this page above left
Flower card
artist's collection
pen and ink
with color markers

this page above right
Moon light
artist's collection
pen and ink
with color markers

this page below right
Flower card
artist's collection
pen and ink
with color markers

this page above right
Japanese girl
artist's collection
pen and ink
with color markers

above left
The pattern of a flower
artist's collection
pen and ink with color markers

above right
Daisy
artist's collection
pen and ink with color markers

below
I want to become the princess
Magazine CAZ
pen and ink with color markers

Pink poodle

Button · Judy and Caren

three daughters

Button

A heel floral design

Three dear shoes

A talkative cup and others

Pu-Pu-Pu

A light is set aglow

Capricorn

Aquarius

Pisces

Sagittarius

Scorpio

Libra

Leo

Virgo

Gemini

Taurus

Aries

Cancer

horoscope

naho **okawa** tokyo

this page
Tokyo furniture shop mag
"an an" magazine
Adobe Photoshop

opposite above
hair salon
"an an" magazine
Adobe Photoshop

opposite right
Tokyo!
"an an" magazine
Adobe Photoshop

this page top left
dating couple
"an an" magazine
Adobe Photoshop

this page top right
men's mind
"an an" magazine
Adobe Photoshop

this page above
anna sui 2002
anna sui
pen and ink

this page right
untitled
artist's collection
Adobe Photoshop

opposite
horoscope
vogue italia bambini magazine
gouche on watercolor paper

above
aloha
artist's collection
Illustrator & Photoshop

below
sketch 01
artist's collection
Illustrator & Photoshop

opposite
bookstore
forbes
Illustrator & Photoshop

hiroshi **fujii** tokyo

© HIROSHI FUJII

haruka **ota** tokyo

this page above left
sepia winter
artist's collection
pencil, Photoshop

this page above right
sepia summer
artist's collection
pencil, Photoshop

this page below left
sepia spring
artist's collection
pencil, Photoshop

this page below right
sepia autumn
artist's collection
pencil, Photoshop

opposite
sayonara when fireworks is over
artist's collection
pencil, Photoshop

wakaba okinawa

above
jump
artist's collection
Pencil & Photoshop

below
japan
artist's collection
Pencil & Photoshop

right
playground
artist's collection
Pencil & Photoshop

this page above
air boy
artist's collection
Pencil & Photoshop

this page left
blindness
artist's collection
Pencil & Photoshop

opposite
birds
artist's collection
Pencil & Photoshop

mifumi **mineta** tokyo

above
kokoro
artist's collection
oil painting

below left
kinoko
artist's collection
oil painting

below right
ouji
artist's collection
oil painting

above left
ai
artist's collection
oil painting

above right
meeko
artist's collection
oil painting

below left
date
artist's collection
oil painting

below right
namida
artist's collection
oil painting

above left
smoke
artist's collection
oil painting

above right
sanpo
artist's collection
oil painting

below left
girl
artist's collection
oil painting

below right
tenshi2
artist's collection
oil painting

above left
rpg 20000
artist's collection
oil painting

above right
fuyu
artist's collection
oil painting

below left
usagi
artist's collection
oil painting

below right
yoake
artist's collection
oil painting

delicatessen cristiana valentini reggio emilia . italy

this page above
autunno italiano
mondofragile
freehand, photoshop

this page below
tempo di primavera
mondofragile
freehand, photoshop

opposite
giappone mon amour
mondofragile
freehand, photoshop

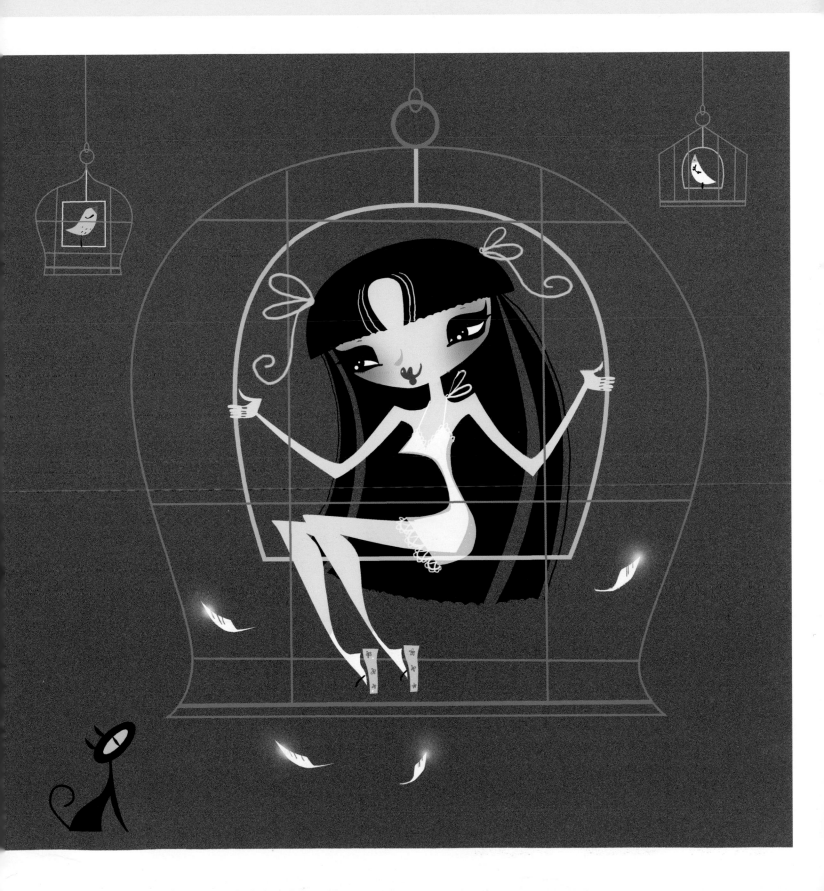

this page
angurie da luigi
mondofragile
freehand, photoshop

opposite
effetto pizza
mondofragile
freehand, photoshop

LA PIZZA
MARGHERITA
MARINARA
NAPOLI
VEGETARIANA
TACCO ALTO
CASA MIA

this page left
divieto di sosta
mondofragile
freehand, photoshop

this page below
effetto shopping
mondofragile
freehand, photoshop

opposite
confetto
mondofragile
freehand, photoshop

dal barbiere
mondofragile
freehand, photoshop

tadahiro uesugi
[1966]
address:
1-6-17#102 Zenpukuji, Suginami-ku,
Tokyo , Japan 167-0041
website:
www10.big.or.jp/~tuesugi/
e-mail:
tuesugi@mail1.big.or.jp
tel & Fax: +81-3-3397-2946

sai tamiya
[1970]
address:
201 Sunrise 2-4-21 Kitamachi Nishitokyo-shi
Tokyo Japan 202-0003
website:
www.asahi-net.or.jp/~bv9s-tmy/sai
e-mail:
bv9s-tmy@asahi-net.or.jp

hitomi nagao
[1980]
address:
Dai-Machi 4-30-9-208 Hachiuji-Shi
Tokyo, 1930931 Japan
website:
http://cherry2.adam.ne.jp
e-mail:
hitomi-n@gk9.so-net.ne.jp

maccosi
nakanishi machiko
[1967]
address:
#603,1-9-1, Azamino, Aoba-ku,
Yokohama, 225-0011 Japan
website:
www.ne.jp/asahi/gallery/maccosi
e-mail:
macco_shi_2000@geocities.co.jp

naomi yuge
[1971]
address:
1-63 Amanishinomachi, Takatsuki-si,
Osaka, 569-1107 JAPAN
website:
www.poronpe.com
e-mail:
mail@poronpe.com

hiroko hasegawa
[1 967]
address:
2-34-15-201,Mejiro,Toshima-ku,
Tokyo, 171-0031 Japan
website:
www.suisen.sakura.ne.jp/~sheep/
e-mail:
sheep@suisen.x0.com
tel: +81-3-5396-6724

yuko yoshioka
[1972]
address:
Mitaka Hills 101, 4-16-27, Shimorenjaku,
Mitaka-shi, Tokyo, 181-0013 Japan
website:
http://www01.u-page.so-net.ne.jp/wb3/yossi/
e-mail:
yossi@wb3.so-net.ne.jp

yuka maeda
[1975]
agent:
dream and more Co. Ltd.,
Kensou Bldg. 5F, 2-13-3, Shimoyamate
St. Chuo-ku, Kobe 650-0011, Japan
e-mail:
info@dream-more.com
Tel.+81-78-327-2155   Fax +81-78-327-2156

emma.mori
[1972]
address:
1-3-4-605 Seishin-cho Edogawa-ku Tokyo
134-0087 Japan
website:
http://member.nifty.ne.jp/emma
e-mail:
emma@mbf.nifty.com

ryutaro odagiri
[1977]
address:
1-1-1-203 Shimohouya,Nishi Tokyo shi
Tokyo 202-0013 Japan
website:
www02.u-page.so-net.ne.jp/wb3/osyare/
e-mail:
osyare@wb3.so-net.ne.jp
tel + Fax: +81 424 38 8522

ringirl
sanae yabussaki
[1978]
address:
948-2 Toyoshiki Kashiwa-shi Chiba-ken,
Japan
website:
www.ringirl.com
e-mail:
kotori@ringirl.com

chinatsu souzen
[1973]
address:
shimofukumoto-cho 7089 B-202
kagoshimashi - 891-0144
website:
www2.synapse.ne.jp/natsunatsu/
e-mail:
natsunatsu@po2.synapse.ne.jp

toru kono
[1970]
address:
1-1-10-#801 Kego, Chuo-ku,Fukuoka-city
810-0023 japan
website:
www.lolo66.com
e-mail:
mail@lolo66.com

yuca shimotashiro
yuca akiyama
[1975]
address:
#204,2-41-50,Higashiarima, Miyamae-ku,
Kawasaki-shi, Kanagawa 216-0002 Japan
website:
http://homepage2.nifty.com/yuca
e-mail:
yuca@mbj.nifty.com

hasebe mamiko
[1974]
address:
3-501 ageo-house,2-82-2 nishimiyashita,
ageo-shi, saitama-ken,
362-0043 japan
website:
http://home8.highway.ne.jp/mmk/
e-mail:
mmk@ph.highway.ne.jp

uyo takayama
[1966]
address:
203,2-12-18,Okusawa, Setagaya-ku,
Tokyo, 150-0083 Japan
website:
www3.cnet-ta.ne.jp/u/uyo
e-mail:
uyo@t.design.co.jp
tel + Fax: +81-3-3718-9012

shiro taniguchi
[1960]
address:
#301 1-1-19 kichijoji-kitamachi Musasino-shi
Tokyo, 180-0001 Japan
website:
http://460s.com
e-mail:
shiro@460s.com
tel + fax: +81-422-20-4630

umezawa button
[1972]
address:
201Feries-Nishiogiita
24-8,Nishiogikita 5chome
Suginami-ku,Tokyo, 167-0042 Japan
website:
www7.ocn.ne.jp/~button
e-mail:
button@io.ocn.ne.jp

naho ogawa
[1975]
address:
2-4-11 Taishido Setagaya-ku
Tokyo 154 Japan
website:
www.naho.com
e-mail:
mail@naho.com
tel: +81 5 5432 3439

hiroshi fujii
[1957]
address:
2-14-27-106 higashi shibuya-ku tokyo
150-0011 Japan
management contact:
CREEK&RIVER Co Ltd.
yokoyama@hq.cri.co.jp
http://www.cri.co.jp/
[rey yokoyama]

haruka ota
[1977]
address:
1-50-10,Sakura,Setagaya-ku,
Tokyo 156-0053 Japan
website:
http://ha-ruka.honesta.net
e-mail:
ha-ruka@honesta.net
tel: +81-904-543-6953

wakaba
[1977]
address:
236-4 Aza Ueyonabaru Yonabarucity,
Okinawa, Japan
website:
www.airily.org
e-mail:
wakaba@ona.att.ne.jp

mineta mifumi
[1975]
website:
http://mizuiromoufu.m78.com
e-mail:
moufu@m78.com

delicatessen
gabriele Fantuzzi [1967]
cristiana valentini [1970]
address:
via che guevara 55, Reggio Emilia, Italy
website:
www.delicatessen.it
e-mail:
info@delica.it
tel: +39 522 293097

you

 maccari, love, © artist's collection, Photoshop

Thanks to: / Grazie a: tadahiro uesugi, sai tamiya, nakanishi machiko, yuka maeda, hitomi nagao, yuko yoshioka, hiroko hasegawa, naomi yuge, emma maruyama, ryutaro odagiri, sanae yabussaki, chinatsu souzen, toru kono, yuca akiyama, hasebe mamiko. haruka ota, uyo takayama, shiro taniguchi, umezawa button, wakaba,naho ogawa, hiroshi fujii, mineta mifuni, azumi sugimoto, rey yokoyama, carlo branzaglia, letizia rustichelli, fabio caleffi@happybooks, manuel majoli, doriano@pico, federica e veronica@inside, filippo@graphiland

printed in italy - ISBN 88-86416-42-3